Preparatory Level

Specific Skill Series

Locating the Answer

Richard A. Boning

Fifth Edition

SRA/McGraw-Hill

Columbus, Ohio

Cover, Back Cover, ZEFA/Germany/The Stock Market

SRA/McGraw-Hill

*A Division of The **McGraw·Hill** Companies*

Send all inquiries to:
    SRA/McGraw-Hill
    8787 Orion Place
    Columbus, OH 43240-4027

ISBN 0-02-687950-6

   8 9 IPC 05 04

To the Teacher

PURPOSE:

As its title indicates, LOCATING THE ANSWER develops pupils' skill in finding *where* sought-for information can be found within a passage. Pupils must carefully read and understand each question, grasp phrase and sentence units, and discriminate between pertinent and irrelevant ideas.

FOR WHOM:

The skill of LOCATING THE ANSWER is developed through a series of books spanning ten levels (Picture, Preparatory, A, B, C, D, E, F, G, H). The Picture Level is for pupils who have not acquired a basic sight vocabulary. The Preparatory Level is for pupils who have a basic sight vocabulary but are not yet ready for the first-grade-level book. Books A through H are appropriate for pupils who can read on levels one through eight, respectively. **The use of the *Specific Skill Series Placement Test* is recommended to determine the appropriate level.**

THE NEW EDITION:

The fifth edition of the *Specific Skill Series* maintains the quality and focus that has distinguished this program for more than 25 years. A key element central to the program's success has been the unique nature of the reading selections. Nonfiction pieces about current topics have been designed to stimulate the interest of students, motivating them to use the comprehension strategies they have learned to further their reading. To keep this important aspect of the program intact, a percentage of the reading selections have been replaced in order to ensure the continued relevance of the subject material.

In addition, a significant percentage of the artwork in the program has been replaced to give the books a contemporary look. The cover photographs are designed to appeal to readers of all ages.

SESSIONS:

Short practice sessions are the most effective. It is desirable to have a practice session every day or every other day, using a few units each session.

To the Teacher

SCORING:

Pupils should record their answers on the reproducible worksheets. The worksheets make scoring easier and provide uniform records of the pupils' work. Using worksheets also avoids consuming the exercise books.

It is important for pupils to know how well they are doing. For this reason, units should be scored as soon as they have been completed. Then a discussion can be held in which pupils justify their choices. (The Integrated Language Activities, many of which are open-ended, do not lend themselves to an objective score; thus there are no answer keys for these pages.)

GENERAL INFORMATION ON *LOCATING THE ANSWER*:

At the earlier levels the answer to the question is worded much the same as the question itself. As the books increase in difficulty, there is less correspondence between the phrasing of the question and the phrasing of the answer.

SUGGESTED STEPS:

1. Pupils read the question *first* and then look for the answer.

2. Pupils use the range finder (sentence choices) in Books B–H. The letters or numbers in the range finder (below the question) indicate which sentences must be read to locate the answer to the question. In the Picture Level, the pupils decide which picture answers the question. For Preparatory and A levels, the number before the question tells the paragraph to read.

3. Pupils read the sentences with the question in mind. (On the Picture Level, pupils look at the pictures. On the Preparatory and A levels, pupils read the paragraph.)

4. When using Books B–H, pupils write (in the space on the worksheet) the letter or number of the sentence that answers the question. On the Picture Level, pupils write the letter of the correct picture choice. On the Preparatory and A levels, pupils write the letter of the correct word choice.

Additional information on using LOCATING THE ANSWER with pupils will be found in the **Specific Skill Series Teacher's Manual**.

RELATED MATERIALS:

Specific Skill Series Placement Tests, which enable the teacher to place pupils at their appropriate levels in each skill, are available for the Elementary (Pre-1–6) and Midway (4–8) grade levels.

About This Book

There are many reasons people read. They read stories just for fun. They read newspapers to find out what is happening in the world. They read ads to help them decide what to buy. They read books to find out about different things.

Reading to find out about things is different from other kinds of reading. First you look quickly to find a page that will give you the answer you want. Then you read carefully. You think about what you want to find out.

It is important to know what to look for when you read to find out about facts. You need to read with your questions in mind. It is like looking for something you have lost. You don't know where the lost thing is, but you know what you are looking for.

In this book, you will read stories. You will answer two questions about each story. Read the questions first. Then look for the answers in the story. The answer to question 1 is in part 1 of the story. The answer to question 2 is in part 2.

A New Friend

1.   Maria went to a new school. She did not know any of the boys and girls. A girl named Ann said hello to Maria.

2.   Soon Ann and Maria were friends. Now Maria was happy. She liked her new friend. She liked going to the new school.

1. Where did Maria go?

   (A) to a store   **(B) to a new school**

2. What did Maria like?

   (A) her new friend   **(B) her old house**

Having Fun

1.   "This is going to be fun," said Bill. He was going for his first ride in an airplane. Bill and his father got into the airplane.

2.   Up, up it went. Bill could see streets and houses. The houses looked very little. Bill said, "I like riding in an airplane."

1. Who went with Bill?

    (A) his father   **(B) a friend**

2. How did the houses look?

    (A) big   **(B) little**

A Goat Ride

1. Kelly went to the farm. She wanted to ride a horse. There was no horse at the farm, but there was a goat.

2. Kelly got on the goat. It took her all around the farm. The goat did not go fast, but Kelly liked the ride.

1. Where did Kelly go?

   (A) to the zoo   **(B) to the farm**

2. What did Kelly ride?

   (A) a horse   **(B) a goat**

Ann's Party

1.   It was Ann's birthday. All her friends came to her party. They had cake to eat, and they played games.

2.   After the party, the children looked at TV. They looked at a very funny show. Ann and her friends had a good time.

1. What did the children do?

   (A) read books   **(B) played games**

2. When did the children look at TV?

   (A) after the party   **(B) before the party**

At the Zoo

1.   The boys went to the zoo. They saw many animals. Some of the animals were big. Some of the animals were little.

2.   When it was time to go, all the boys got balloons. They took the balloons home. The boys said, "It is fun going to the zoo."

1. What did the boys see?

   (A) a train   **(B) animals**

2. What did the boys take home?

   (A) food   **(B) balloons**

Going to School

1.   Kate rides a bus to school. The school is a long way from her house. Many of Kate's friends ride on the bus, too.

2.   Kate and her friends have a good time on the bus. They sing, tell stories, and play games. They all like riding the bus to school.

1. Who rides to school with Kate?

    (A) her friends   **(B) her sister**

2. What does Kate do on the bus?

    (A) reads books   **(B) plays games**

Things at the Zoo

Animal Homes	Places for Help
Monkey Cage	First-Aid Stand
Sea Lion Pond	Food Stand
Deer Park	Rest Rooms
Lion Den	Ticket Stand

Fun-Rides Park is in back of the Food Stand.

A. Exercising Your Skill

You are on a trip to the zoo. The sign above is at the main gate. It lists what is at the zoo. Think about the places on the sign. On your paper, write the answers to these questions.

1. Where would you buy lunch? _____
2. Where would you see baby deer? _____
3. Where would you get a bandage? _____

B. Expanding Your Skill

Where would you go to find the things in the box? On your paper, write the answer. Then add two more things to the list.

merry-go-round	roller coaster	bumper cars

C. Exploring Language

Listen to the story about the zoo. Fill in the blanks. Find the answers in the sign in Part A.

Going to the zoo is fun! First, we buy our tickets at the ＿＿. Then we watch the baby lion cubs at the ＿＿. At noon, we buy pizza from the ＿＿. Then we walk in back of the Food Stand to find ＿＿. A day at the zoo is great!

D. Expressing Yourself

Do one of these things.

1. Draw a map of the zoo. Be sure to put in all the places listed on the sign. Use large paper if you can.

2. Pretend you are taking a trip to the zoo. Tell what you will do on your trip. Use the sign to help you plan your day.

Looking for Tom

1.   "Go away, and I will try to find you," said Ken. Tom ran around the house. Ken went to look for him.

2.   Ken looked and looked, but he could not find Tom. At last, Tom called, "Look up here." Ken looked up into the tree. There was Tom.

1. Where did Tom run?

   (A) around the house   **(B) down the street**

2. Where was Tom?

   (A) in a tree   **(B) in a car**

A New Pet

1. Kim was not happy. Her dog had run away. She did not have a pet to play with.

2. That night, Kim's mother gave her a big box. Kim said, "I hear something in the box." She looked and saw a baby duck. Kim was happy to have a new pet.

1. What had run away?

   (A) Kim's cat   **(B) Kim's dog**

2. What was Kim's new pet?

   (A) a duck   **(B) a rabbit**

A Ride Home

1.   Bill was walking home from school. It began to rain. Bill ran under a tree but still got wet.

2.   A car stopped by the tree. "Do you want a ride?" a man asked. It was Father. Bill got into the car, and they went home.

1. Where did Bill run?

    (A) to school   **(B) under a tree**

2. Who gave Bill a ride?

    (A) Mother   **(B) Father**

Time for Bed

1. "Where is Rosa?" asked Mother. "It is time for her to go to bed." No one had seen Rosa for a long time.

2. Mother looked out the window. There was Rosa. She was sleeping under a tree. "Come in, Rosa," called Mother. "You should sleep in bed, not under a tree."

1. Who was Mother looking for?

    (A) Rosa   **(B) Mary**

2. What was Rosa doing?

    (A) playing   **(B) sleeping**

A Boy Paints

1.   Rob wanted to paint something. He asked Father, "May I paint the house?" Father told Rob that he was too little to paint the house.

2.   "Paint your old wagon," said Father. He gave Rob some red paint. Rob had fun painting his wagon.

1. What did Rob want to paint?

   (A) his bike   **(B) the house**

2. What did Rob paint?

   (A) his wagon   **(B) a boat**

A Surprise

1.   Father was not home. Pam said, "I will surprise Father. I will cut the grass."

2.   Pam cut the grass. When Father came home, he was surprised. Father said, "Thank you for cutting the grass. Now I will not have to do it."

1. Who did Pam want to surprise?

   (A) Mother   **(B) Father**

2. What did Father say to Pam?

   (A) "Go to bed"   **(B) "Thank you"**

Want Ads: Pets for Sale	
CATS Want a Cat? See Us Soon **Kitty Pet Store**	DOGS Come to the **Puppy Pet Store** We Have Dogs for You All Dog Things Too— Food, Dog Toys, Bowls
GERBILS Come to **Al's Pets** We Have Baby Gerbils	RABBITS Call 555–1212

A. Exercising Your Skill

Pretend that you want to get a pet. Think about the Want Ads carefully. On your paper, write the answers to these questions.

1. What number would you call to get a rabbit?
2. What would you find at **Al's Pets**?
3. Where would you go to get a kitten?

B. Expanding Your Skill

You have just gotten a puppy. Now you need the things listed in the box below. Use the Want Ads. On your paper, write where you would buy these things. Then add two things to the list.

puppy food	toy bone	water dish

C. Exploring Language

Listen to the story. Use your own words to finish the sentences. Find the answers in the Want Ads in Part A.

My parents said we could get a pet! First, we'll go to Al's Pets to look at ＿＿. Then we'll go to the ＿＿ to look at puppies. Maybe a rabbit would be nice. We'll find out about rabbits. We'll call ＿＿. What kind of pet do you think we should get?

D. Expressing Yourself

Do one of these things.

1. You are going to get a pet. Plan a day visiting pet stores. Use the Want Ads to help you. Make a list of the kinds of pets you want to see and where to see them. Write a story about your day.

2. Pretend that you are getting a puppy today. Write down four things that you need to get ready for the puppy. Then write a name for your new puppy.

A Fire

1.   Patty ran into the house. "Mother!" she called. "Our car is on fire!" Mother ran out to look.

2.   The car was not on fire. It was an old box by the car that was on fire. Mother put water on it. Soon the fire was out.

1. Where did Patty run?

   (A) into the house   **(B) to the store**

2. What was on fire?

   (A) the house   **(B) a box**

Rick and His Cat

1.   "I hear something," said Rick. He looked under his bed. There was his pet cat. It was playing with Rick's toy truck.

2.   Rick put the truck on his bed. The cat jumped on the bed, too. Rick and his cat had fun playing with the toy truck.

1. Where did Rick look?

   (A) at the TV   **(B) under the bed**

2. What did Rick and his cat play with?

   (A) a toy truck   **(B) a red ball**

A Funny Game

1.   Andy and Jean were playing a funny game. Andy made a funny face. Jean smiled but did not laugh.

2.   Then Andy stuck one hand on his nose and pushed it up. He made a face. Jean tried not to laugh, but she could not help it. She began to laugh very hard.

1. Who made a funny face?

   (A) Andy   (B) Jean

2. Where did Andy stick his hand?

   (A) on his nose   (B) over his eye

A Call for Help

1.   "Help! Help!" called Dan. He was up in a tree and could not get down. Dan did not want to fall.

2.   Mother ran to the tree. She helped Dan get down. "Thank you," said Dan. "I will never go up into the tree again."

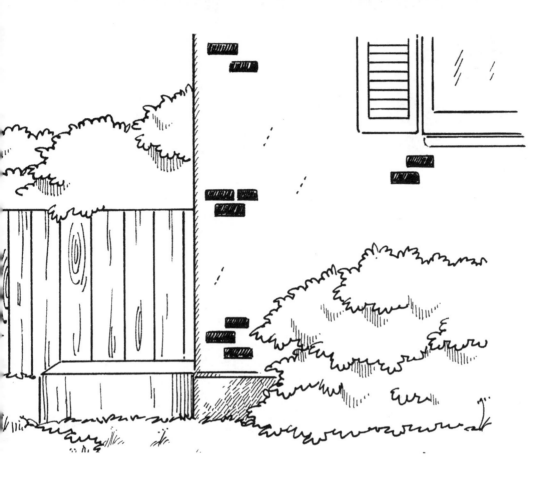

1. Where was Dan?

   (A) in the house   **(B) in a tree**

2. Who helped Dan?

   (A) Mother   **(B) Mary**

A Day at the Lake

1.　　It was too hot to stay inside! Lisa wanted to go swimming, but she could not find her friends.

2.　　Lisa went to the lake alone. When she got there, she found that all her friends had gone swimming, too!

1. What did Lisa want to do?

   (A) play inside   **(B) go swimming**

2. Where did Lisa go?

   (A) to the park   **(B) to the lake**

Building Houses

1. Father likes to go to work. He builds new houses. One day Tim went to work with Father. He helped to build a house.

2. Tim liked working with Father. It was fun helping to build a house. When Tim gets older, he wants to build new houses, too.

1. Where did Father take Tim?

   (A) to work   **(B) to school**

2. What did Tim have fun doing?

   (A) reading a book   **(B) building a house**

A Pet Show

1. The children went to Amy's house. They took their pets with them. They were going to have a pet show.

2. Ken had a dog. José had a rabbit. Amy had a duck. The children had their pets do tricks. It was a good pet show.

1. Where did the children go?

   (A) to a farm   **(B) to Amy's house**

2. What was José's pet?

   (A) a rabbit   **(B) a duck**

Sandwiches	
Turkey	$2.50
Tuna	$2.50
Ham	$2.00

Pizza		Drinks	
Cheese	$3.00	Juice	75¢
Peppers	$3.50	Milk	75¢
Mushrooms	$3.50		

A. Exercising Your Skill

Pretend that you are having lunch at a restaurant. Think about the foods listed on the menu above. On your paper, answer these questions.

1. How much does a ham sandwich cost?
2. How many kinds of pizza can you buy?
3. What two things can you have to drink?

B. Expanding Your Skill

Listen to the names of the foods listed in the box. Could you get these foods at the restaurant talked about in Part A? On your paper, list the things from the box that you could eat there.

Cheese Pizza	Tuna Sandwich	Tea

C. Exploring Language

Listen to each story. On your paper, answer the questions. Find the answers on the menu in Part A.

1. "I'm starved," said Katie, reading the menu. "I really want to eat pizza for lunch. But I don't like mushrooms or peppers at all."

    What kind of pizza should Katie order?

2. "I'm thirsty. I need a drink badly," said Peter to his friends. "I wonder if I can have orange juice?"

    Can Peter have orange juice with his lunch?

D. Expressing Yourself

Do one of these things.

1. Pretend that you are eating lunch at a restaurant. With one or two of your classmates, act out going to the restaurant, ordering your food, eating your meal, and then leaving. One of you can pretend to be the waiter.

2. Draw a picture of a lunch you might have at a restaurant. Use the menu in Part A to help you.

Eating Good Food

1.   "It's time to eat," called Father. Lucy ran into the house. She liked dinner time.

2.   Lucy sat at the table. Father said that Lucy's brother had made the food. Lucy did not want to eat it. Then she tried the food and was surprised. She liked it!

1. Where did Lucy run?

   (A) out of the house   **(B) into the house**

2. Who made the food?

   (A) Lucy's brother   **(B) Lucy's father**

A Lost Pet

1.   Maria went into the house. She wanted to play with her pet cat. Maria called and called, but her cat did not come.

2.   "Where can my cat be?" asked Maria. She looked all around the house. At last, she looked under her bed. There was her cat, playing with a ball.

1. What did Maria have for a pet?

   (A) a cat   **(B) a dog**

2. Where did Maria find her pet?

   (A) at school   **(B) under a bed**

Wendy Stays Home

1.   The girls went to call for Wendy. They wanted to play with her. Wendy told the girls that she did not want to play today.

2.   Wendy sat down with her new book. It was about a lost dog. Wendy said, "It is more fun to read my book than to play with the girls."

UNIT 22

1. What did the girls want to do?

   (A) work   **(B) play**

2. What was Wendy's book about?

   (A) a boat   **(B) a dog**

Going Fishing

1.   Luis and his father went out in a boat. They wanted to catch some fish. Soon they had many fish.

2.   When they got home, Luis told his mother and sister about catching the fish. Luis' sister said, "The next time you go fishing, I want to go, too."

1. Who went fishing with Father?

   (A) Luis   **(B) Bill**

2. What did Luis' sister want to do?

   (A) stay home   **(B) go fishing**

A Bike Ride

1.   Diane got on her bike and went down the street. She was going to her friend's house. It was a long ride, but Diane liked it.

2.   After playing with her friend, Diane got on her bike and went home. The next day, Diane's friend came to her house to play.

1. Where did Diane go?

   (A) to a store   **(B) to a friend's house**

2. What did Diane and her friend do?

   (A) painted   **(B) played**

A Funny Cat

1.　　Mike looked out the window. It was raining. "What can I do to have fun?" asked Mike.

2.　　Then Mike saw his cat. He put a hat on the cat. He put a little coat on the cat. Mike had fun with his funny cat.

1. What did Mike see out the window?

   (A) the sun   **(B) rain**

2. What did Mike put on his cat?

   (A) a hat   **(B) shoes**

> **Your School Day**
>
> Hour 1: Math Hour 4: Science
> Hour 2: Reading RECESS
> Hour 3: Music Hour 5: Gym
>   LUNCH TIME

A. Exercising Your Skill

It is your first day of school. Think about what will happen during the day. On your paper, answer these questions.

1. What do you learn about in the first hour?
2. What do you do right after recess?
3. After which class do you eat lunch?

B. Expanding Your Skill

Listen to the words in the box. In which class would you do all these things? Which hour would you go there? Add one more thing you might do at that class.

> basketball   kickball   races

C. Exploring Language

Listen to these stories. On your paper, write the answer to each question. Find the answers in Part A.

1. "I've been thinking about that story all weekend," said Jill. "I can't wait until the next class so that we can all read together." What class is Jill waiting for? _____

2. "What did you bring for lunch?" Sam said to Ben. "I'm hungry! After this class, we can eat!"
   Where are Sam and Ben now? _____

D. Expressing Yourself

Do one of these things.

1. Write a story about your school day. Tell what you like to do best.

2. Pretend that you are the principal of a school. Write down all the things you would plan for your students each day. You can plan anything you like, even three hours of recess a day!